TOUCHSTONE

MICHAEL McCARTHY
JEANNE McCARTEN
HELEN SANDIFORD

WITH

LISA HUTCHINS
JENNIFER WILKIN

4B

WORKBOOK

CAMBRIDGE
UNIVERSITY PRESS

CAMBRIDGE UNIVERSITY PRESS
Cambridge, New York, Melbourne, Madrid, Cape Town, Singapore, São Paulo

Cambridge University Press
32 Avenue of the Americas, New York, NY 10013-2473, USA

www.cambridge.org
Information on this title: www.cambridge.org/9780521601481

First published 2006

Printed in Hong Kong, China, by Golden Cup Printing Company, Limited

A catalog record for this publication is available from the British Library

ISBN-13   978-0-521-66593-3 pack consisting of student's book and self-study audio CD/CD-ROM (Windows®, Mac®)
ISBN-10   0-521-66593-0 pack consisting of student's book and self-study audio CD/CD-ROM (Windows®, Mac®)

ISBN-13   978-0-521-60144-3 pack consisting of student's book/Korea and self-study audio CD/CD-ROM (Windows®, Mac®)
ISBN-10   0-521-60144-4 pack consisting of student's book/Korea and self-study audio CD/CD-ROM (Windows®, Mac®)

ISBN-13   978-0-521-60145-0 pack consisting of student's book A and self-study audio CD/CD-ROM (Windows®, Mac®)
ISBN-10   0-521-60145-2 pack consisting of student's book A and self-study audio CD/CD-ROM (Windows®, Mac®)

ISBN-13   978-0-521-60146-7 pack consisting of student's book B and self-study audio CD/CD-ROM (Windows®, Mac®)
ISBN-10   0-521-60146-0 pack consisting of student's book B and self-study audio CD/CD-ROM (Windows®, Mac®)

ISBN-13   978-0-521-66592-6 workbook
ISBN-10   0-521-66592-2 workbook

ISBN-13   978-0-521-60147-4 workbook A
ISBN-10   0-521-60147-9 workbook A

ISBN-13   978-0-521-60148-1 workbook B
ISBN-10   0-521-60148-7 workbook B

ISBN-13   978-0-521-66591-9 teacher's edition
ISBN-10   0-521-66591-4 teacher's edition

ISBN-13   978-0-521-66588-9 CDs (audio)
ISBN-10   0-521-66588-4 CDs (audio)

ISBN-13   978-0-521-66589-6 cassettes
ISBN-10   0-521-66589-2 cassettes

Art direction, book design, photo research, and layout services: Adventure House, NYC

Contents

Unit 7 Problem solving

Getting things done

1 Get someone else on the job!

Grammar Read each sentence. Then circle the correct verbs to complete the sentences.

1. Anita never **gets** / **has** a mechanic check her oil. She just **gets** / **has** her brother to do it.

2. Tony always **gets** / **has** someone at the copy shop make his copies.

3. When Midori sold her small house, she **got** / **had** a famous architect design and build her a new one.

4. Emilio hates doing the dishes, so he **gets** / **has** his little sister to do them.

2 Get a professional.

Grammar Complete the radio advertisements with the correct forms of the verbs.

1. When your car is dirty, get a professional __to wash__ (wash) it at Jake's Car Wash. Cheap prices. Friendly service. Get your car __washed__ (wash) at Jake's today!

2. Have you always done your own decorating or gotten a friend _____ (do) it? This spring, why not have your home _____ (redecorate) by Paint Works? No job too big or too small.

3. Need a new image? Come to Alice's Salon to have your hair _____ (cut) by an expert. Get our stylists _____ (help) you choose the style that's right for you.

4. Don't pay a fortune to have your car _____ (repair). When your car breaks down, call Joe's Garage and get it _____ (fix) for less.

5. With your busy lifestyle, you don't have time for chores. From now on, get Helping Hands _____ (do) them for you. Whether you want to have the whole house _____ (clean) or just some shirts _____ (iron), we're here to help.

3 Get some advice online.

Grammar   Jerry just moved to a new city. He posted these questions on an online
bulletin board. Complete the answers with the pairs of words in the box.
Add appropriate pronouns.

get / clean	have / deliver	have / paint
✓get / repair	have / fix	

Bulletin Board

Jerry85   My camera's making a funny noise. I can't afford a new one.
          Does anyone repair cameras these days?

StanP   You can ___*get it repaired*___ at Mick's Repairs. They're
          pretty cheap.

Jerry85   My TV's not working. Can someone recommend a good shop?

LilyRose I like Gus's TV Shop. It won't cost a lot to _____ there.

Jerry85   Help! I need to find a really good dry cleaner's. I spilled spaghetti
          sauce all over my silk shirt last night.

JuanJ   When my clothes are stained, I always _____ at
          Main Street Cleaners. It's expensive, but they do a great job.

Jerry85   Where can I buy really fresh fruit and vegetables near Fry Street?

Hwatanabe There's a health-food store on the corner of Fry and Middle Streets.
          You can also buy your groceries online and _____ .

Jerry85   My apartment needs painting. Does anyone know a
          professional painter?

Psmith89 It will cost a lot to _____ professionally. Could you paint it
          yourself?

4 About you

Grammar
and
vocabulary   Answer the questions with true information.

1. What's something you usually pay to have someone do for you?

   __I usually pay to have someone fix my motorbike._____

2. What's something you get a family member to do for you?

   _____

3. How much does it cost to get your hair cut?

   _____

4. What's something you would have done by a professional?

   _____

5. What's the last thing you had repaired?

   _____

6. If your cell phone were broken, would you get it fixed or buy a new one?

   _____

What needs to be done?

1 What's wrong?

Vocabulary | Choose the best word to complete April's thoughts.

1. The mouse isn't working. I'll have to (**recharge**) / **fix** the battery.
2. I should really **tighten** / **upgrade** this software. I don't have the latest version.
3. Something's wrong with the monitor. I've tried **adjusting** / **replacing** the controls, but it's just not right.
4. Or maybe I need to **recharge** / **tighten** the plug.
5. If the computer can't be fixed, I wonder if the store will **replace** / **adjust** it.

2 A fixer-upper

Grammar and vocabulary | Brent's new house needs a lot of work. Find eight problems in the picture. Write a sentence with *need* + verb + *-ing* or a sentence with *need* + passive infinitive to suggest a solution. Use the verbs in the box.

adjust
clean
fix
paint
repair
replace
throw away
✓ tighten

1. The light keeps flickering. It needs to be tightened.
2. _____
3. _____
4. _____
5. _____
6. _____
7. _____
8. _____

3 Leaks and dents

Vocabulary | Complete the conversations with the words and phrases in the box.

dead	get a shock	making a funny noise	torn
✓dent	hole	slow	won't turn on
fall off	leaking	stain	
flickering	loose	stopped	

1. *A* What happened to your car? There's a big _____ **dent** _____ in the door.
   And look, the oil is _____ .
   B Well, I was driving to school, and the car started _____ .
   So, I pulled over to the side of the road and hit a tree by accident.

2. *A* What happened? You're 15 minutes late.
   B Am I? My watch must be _____ . Uh-oh. It looks like it's
   _____ .

3. *A* Oh, no! The computer's not working. It's completely _____ .
   B You know, yesterday the screen kept _____ on and off.
   A Well, now it _____ at all. Maybe I should check the cables.
   B OK. Just be careful. You don't want to _____ .

4. *A* I had a horrible day. First, I spilled coffee on my new jeans.
   B Ooh. I bet that left a terrible _____ .
   A It did. Then, on the way home from work, I tripped and fell. Now my pants are
   stained, *and* they have a big _____ in them.
   B Well, _____ jeans are fashionable right now!

5. *A* Look at this old cabinet I found. I think I can fix it up nicely.
   B Really? All the knobs are _____ . And the legs – they all look like
   they're about to _____ . Are you sure you can fix it?
   A Oh, yeah. I repair furniture all the time.

4 About you

Grammar | Write true answers. Use *need* + verb + *-ing* or *need* + passive infinitive.

1. What's something in your home that needs cleaning?
   My kitchen always needs cleaning.

2. What's something in your home that needs to be tightened sometimes?
   _____

3. What's something in your home that sometimes needs to be adjusted?
   _____

4. What's something you own that needs to be recharged?
   _____

5. What's something you own that needs replacing?
   _____

1 Like it?

Conversation strategies

A Match each sentence with its shorter version.

1. Do you like it? __d__
2. I'm ready! _____
3. I'd love to! _____
4. Do you want me to help you? _____
5. Do you need some help moving it? _____
6. Do you want me to get it? _____
7. Do you want one? _____
8. Have you got any chips? _____
9. Are you ready? _____

a. Want me to help?
b. Ready?
c. Want one?
d. Like it?
e. Ready!
f. Got any chips?
g. Need some help moving it?
h. Want me to get it?
i. Love to!

B Complete the conversations with the shorter sentences from part A.

1. *A* Oh, that looks heavy. _Need some help moving it?_

   B No. I think I can carry it by myself. But thanks anyway.

2. *A* _____

   B Yes. I'm all ready to go.

   A Wow. That's a beautiful dress!

   B _____

   A Yeah, I really do!

3. *A* Gosh, I'm hungry. _____

   B No, but I have some cookies. _____

   A Sure. Thanks.

4. *A* Oh, I can't figure out how to use this new computer program.

   B _____

   A Oh, yeah. That would be great!

5. *A* Oh, there's the phone. I'm busy washing the dishes.

   B _____

   A Yes, please. Could you just take a message? Thanks.

6. *A* Are you hungry? Want to get some sushi?

   B _____

   A Great. Are you ready to go now?

   B Yeah. _____

2 Ooh!

Conversation strategies

Circle the best word to begin each sentence.

1. **Ooh!** / **Ouch!** I see why it isn't working!

2. **Yuck!** / **Ow!** That hurt!

3. **Ugh!** / **Whoops!** I poured too much!

4. **Yuck!** / **Oops!** This tastes awful!

5. **Shoot!** / **Ouch!** I missed the bus.

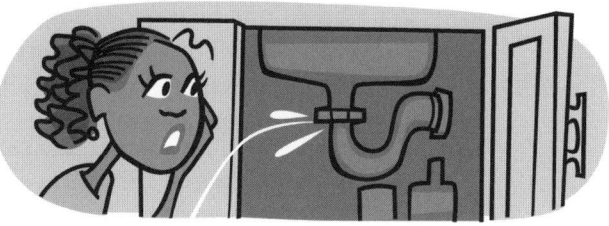

6. **Uh-oh!** / **Whoops!** The sink is leaking.

3 Scrambled conversations

Conversation strategies

Number the lines of the conversations in the correct order.

1. _____ OK, put it down. How does it look?
   __1__ Need some help moving the table?
   _____ Hmm. Don't like it there. Let's move it back.
   _____ Yes, please. It's heavy. I can't move it by myself.
   _____ Ready. OK. . . . Ooh! . . . It's heavy.
   _____ OK. Let's lift it together. Ready?

2. _____ How about that new horror movie – *Monster Girl*?
   _____ Love to. What movie do you want to see?
   _____ OK. What time is it playing?
   _____ Too bad! Want to go out for dessert instead?
   _____ Let me check. Shoot! We just missed the 7:00 show.
   _____ Want to go to the movies tonight?

1 Brainteasers

Reading **A** Read the puzzles. How many can you answer without looking at the solutions?

Here are some problems to solve, just for fun!

1. There are 20 people in an otherwise empty room. Each person can see everything in the room without moving in any way (other than his or her eyes). Where can you place an apple so that all but one person can see it?

2. A man was taking a walk outside when it started to rain. He didn't have an umbrella, and he wasn't wearing a hat. When he got home, his clothes were soaked, but not a single hair on his head got wet. How is this possible?

3. A painting hangs on the wall at a person's house. When the person is asked who is in the painting, the person replies, "I don't have a brother or a sister, but my mother's daughter is that man's mother." Who is the portrait of?

4. How can you throw a ball so that it reverses direction and comes back to you without bouncing off or touching any other object?

5. If it takes two men four hours to dig a hole, how much time does it take them to dig half a hole?

6. You are walking through a field, and you find something to eat. It doesn't have legs, and it doesn't have meat. You take it home and put it someplace warm. Three days later, it gets up and walks away. What is it?

7. Rearrange these letters into one long word: doornonegwl

B Match each puzzle above with its solution.

a. "one long word"   7
b. Throw it straight up in the air. ____
c. The man is bald. ____
d. An egg. ____
e. The owner's son. ____
f. On someone's head. ____
g. You can't dig half a hole! ____

C Find these words and expressions in the puzzles. Match them with their definitions.

1. (puzzle 1) but   c
2. (puzzle 2) soaked ____
3. (puzzle 2) not a single ____
4. (puzzle 3) portrait ____
5. (puzzle 4) reverses direction ____
6. (puzzle 4) bouncing off ____

a. not one
b. hitting something and moving away quickly
c. except
d. a painting of a person
e. goes in the opposite direction
f. very wet

2 *Interesting proposal*

Writing **A** Read the proposal below. Circle the problem. Underline the solution and benefits. Then put parentheses ( ) around how the solution will be implemented.

I find that there is sometimes a lack of understanding and respect between students and teachers.

In order to solve this problem, we should have a teacher-student swap day once a semester. On this day, students would be the teachers and teachers would be the students. The reason for this is so that students and teachers can learn from the challenges the others face. This could benefit the school in several ways. First, students could see what teachers have to do to prepare for a class. Second, teachers could learn new ideas from students and how students learn best. Another advantage would be that students could find out if teaching is something they'd like to do as a career.

This could be easily put into practice. Each semester, every teacher would become a student and let two students take over the class – one in the morning and one in the afternoon. Students who are interested would volunteer to teach a subject they feel comfortable with. They would then be chosen at random.

B Write about a solution to a problem. Explain its benefits and how it can be implemented. Use these ideas or your own.

- Too much litter in the city
- Not enough opportunities to practice English outside the classroom
- Ineffective public transportation

Unit 7 Progress chart

Mark the boxes below to rate your progress. ✔ = I know how to . . .　　? = I need to review how to . . .	To review, go back to these pages in the Student's Book.
Grammar	
☐ make sentences using causative *get* and *have*	66 and 67
☐ use *need* + passive infinitive and *need* + verb + *-ing*	68 and 69
Vocabulary	
☐ use 5 new verbs to talk about fixing problems	68
☐ use at least 10 new expressions to describe everyday problems	69
Conversation strategies	
☐ use "shorter sentences" in informal conversations	70
☐ use at least 6 expressions when things go wrong	71
Writing	
☐ present a solution to a problem	73

Unit 8 Behavior

Reactions

1 It's not nice to sulk.

Vocabulary What are these people doing? Write sentences using the words and expressions in the box.

| hang up | hug | laugh out loud | lose his temper | ✓sulk | yell |

1. _He's sulking._   2. _____   3. _____

4. _____   5. _____   6. _____

2 I wouldn't have yelled at him.

Grammar and vocabulary Read each comment. Say what you would have done and what you wouldn't have done. Use the ideas in Exercise 1, or add your own.

1. "Last night, a guy cut in line and bought the last two tickets for the movie I wanted to see!"

   I would have been annoyed. I wouldn't have yelled at him, though.

2. "Yesterday, my aunt gave me $100 for my birthday."

   _____

3. "My best friend told me a really funny joke in the middle of science class."

   _____

4. "Last week, I failed my math exam."

   _____

5. "My little brother spilled a can of soda on my English homework."

   _____

3 What would you have done?

Grammar

A Complete the conversations with past modals *would(n't) have*, *should(n't) have*, or *could(n't) have* and the verbs given. Sometimes more than one answer is possible.

1. *Kai* My aunt gave me this sweater for my birthday. It's not really my taste.

   Sen Well, I agree. . . . It *is* pretty weird. You _could have taken_ (take) it back to the store by now!

   Kai She made it herself, so I can't. And anyway, I _____ (not / do) that. She's so sweet. I _____ (not / want) to upset her.

   Sen Well, maybe you _____ (smile) and said thank you.

   Kai That's exactly what I did! It's the only thing I _____ (do). I _____ (not / say) anything else!

   Sen That's true.

2. *Luz* You know, Cora was supposed to come to my party last weekend, and she never showed up. I was a bit upset.

   Jon Yeah, I think I _____ (be) upset, too.

   Luz I was, but I guess _____ (call) her to see if she was coming.

   Jon Maybe. But she still _____ (contact) you. Although maybe she was sick and couldn't call.

   Luz Yeah, I didn't think about that. But she _____ (get) her mother to call and tell me. That's what I _____ (do).

   Jon Yeah, but you never know. Why don't you call and find out what happened?

B Write questions with past modals that Kai and Luz could have asked in the conversations in part A. Then write your own answers.

Questions   **Answers**

Conversation 1

1. What else / I / say ?

   What else could I have said?   _____

2. How / you / react ?

   _____   _____

3. you / give / it back ?

   _____   _____

Conversation 2

4. you / feel / angry ?

   _____   _____

5. you / call her ?

   _____   _____

6. What / Cora / do ?

   _____   _____

Emotional intelligence

1 What's your personality?

Vocabulary Read what each person says about himself or herself. Write three words that best describe each person.

| aggressive | decisive | flexible | honest | jealous | sensitive |
| confident | determined | ✓happy | impulsive | realistic | sympathetic |

1. I enjoy life. I'm pretty easygoing. If my friends want to do something, I'll usually go along with their plans, unless they're really crazy. I know what I'm capable and not capable of.

   _____happy_____   _____   _____

2. My friends often call me when something is worrying them. They say I'm a good listener, and I always tell them the truth. I don't like to see my friends upset or depressed.

   _____   _____   _____

3. I'm a pretty motivated person. I always know what I want. Once I decide to do something, I do it. I always try my hardest to achieve my goals.

   _____   _____   _____

4. What are my worst qualities? Well, I always want things that other people have. I sometimes lose my temper in stores and can shout if I don't get what I want. I guess I often do things without thinking about the consequences.

   _____   _____   _____

2 Positive or negative?

Vocabulary Which words have a positive meaning for you, and which ones have a negative meaning? Complete the chart with the words in the box.

aggression	determination	happiness	motivation	sensitivity
anger	flexibility	hate	realism	shame
✓confidence	grief	honesty	sadness	sympathy
depression	guilt	jealousy	self-discipline	worry

Positive		Negative	
confidence			

3 She must have!

Rewrite the sentences in parentheses. Use past modals *must have*, *may have*, *might have*, or *could have*. Sometimes more than one answer is possible.

1. A There's no answer. <u>She must have left by now.</u>
                                  (I bet she left by now.)

   B Do you think she's coming by bus?

   A Um, I don't know. _____
                                (Maybe she decided to drive.)

   B I don't think so. Her car's broken down. It was in the garage last night.

   _____
      (It's not possible she got it back yet.)

2. A Did I tell you someone robbed Dana last week and stole her purse?

   B How awful! _____
                         (I bet she was scared.)

   A Well, she was scared at first. The funny thing was, she knew the thief. She went to school with him! But Dana looks really different now. _____
                    (So it's possible he didn't recognize her.)

   B Did she tell him that she knew him?

   A _____ I don't really know.
              (Maybe she told him.)

   B Well, I hope she reported him to the police!

4 About you

Read each situation. Use past modals to complete the sentences with possible reasons why these situations happened.

1. Your roommate overslept and missed an important meeting at work.

   She could <u>have stayed up too late the night before</u> .

   She might <u>not have set her alarm clock</u> .

2. Your best friend hasn't called you in a week.

   He / She may _____ .

   He / She couldn't _____ .

3. Your grandparents forgot your birthday.

   They may not _____ .

   They might _____ .

4. Your sister can't find her favorite CD.

   She must _____ .

   She could _____ .

Speaking of rude people, . . .

1 Rude behavior

Conversation strategies | **Complete the conversation with the expressions in the box.**

I had a similar thing happen to me,	That's like
✓ I had that happen to me	That reminds me of the time
That happened to my friend Nancy,	Speaking of

A She just cut in front of us! It drives me crazy when people do that.

B _I had that happen to me_ last week. Same thing. This woman in the store just pushed her cart right in front of me. I looked at her, and she was like, "Too bad." She was so rude.

A Don't you hate that? _____ people who push right past you in the street. You know, when it's busy. It can really hurt.

B I know. _____ a guy walked right into me on Main Street. He never even apologized.

A Wasn't he looking?

B I guess not. Has that ever happened to you – someone walking directly into you?

A Well, not quite. I mean, _____ but with a door – and I walked into *it*!

B No way! _____ too. She walked into a glass door and knocked herself out! She was in a hurry and wasn't looking where she was going.

A _____ being in a hurry, I have to get going myself. I'll see you tomorrow!

2 Like, what?

Conversation strategies | **Read the sentences. Which meaning of *like* is used?**

a. to give an example   d. to report what someone said
b. to highlight something   e. to say "approximately"
c. to say something is similar

1. I've known Giovanni for like 10 years. _e_
2. My mom asked me to look for her car keys, and I was like, "Again!?" ____
3. I'm always like so tired in the morning, and it's so hard to get out of bed. ____
4. I'm just like my father – we're both tall, athletic, and easygoing. ____
5. My little sister loves TV. Like, she's always watching cartoons or game shows. ____
6. I've been studying for like weeks so that I do well on my final exams. ____
7. I wanted to leave work early tonight, but my boss was like, "You can't leave until you finish your report." ____
8. I'm always forgetting things. Like, I went to the supermarket the other day, and I forgot what I was supposed to buy! ____

3 I was like, "I'm sorry."

Conversation strategies

What does each speaker say next? Write the letter.

1. One of my friends is really sensitive. _d_
2. My sister forgot to call me again. _____
3. My aunt is pretty old. _____
4. My mom is like really impulsive. _____
5. My friend is very motivated, just like me. _____
6. A co-worker got so upset with me. _____

a. She like never remembers!
b. She's like 80 years old!
c. We're both determined to do well in school.
d. Like, she's always crying about nothing.
e. I was like, "I'm sorry. I didn't realize."
f. Like, she does things without thinking.

4 Like, I had a similar experience!

Conversation strategies

Respond to each statement, and describe a similar experience. Use the expressions in the box. Can you add a sentence using *like* with one of the meanings in Exercise 2 on page 62?

I had that happen to me.
That happened to me.
I had a similar experience.
That reminds me (of) . . .
That's like . . .
Speaking of . . . ,

1. I went to a new barber, and he did a terrible job with my hair. I looked ridiculous.

   I had a similiar experience at the hairdreser last year. I asked for curly hair, and when I left, I looked terrible.

2. Someone selling magazine subscriptions called while I was eating dinner last night.

   _____
   _____
   _____

3. I was supposed to meet a friend at the movies last night, but she never showed up.

   _____
   _____
   _____

4. Last night I was at this restaurant, and a man at a table near me talked on his cell phone the whole time.

   _____
   _____
   _____

5. I have a friend who always interrupts me when I tell a story. It drives me crazy.

   _____
   _____
   _____

1 I'm peeved!

Reading **A** Read the blogs. What do the two stories have in common?

☐ The problems were solved by yelling at the person.
☐ Both bloggers yelled at someone.

☐ The problems weren't solved.
☐ Both bloggers feel better for taking action.

Pet Peeves

Pet Peeves

We asked our bloggers to write in with their pet peeves and tell us how they deal with the things that annoy them the most.

Margaret, 32, Ottawa If there's one thing that upsets me, it's people who throw their trash on the street. It really makes me angry when I see people toss their food wrappers and empty soda cans on the sidewalk. They should be ashamed of themselves, but people don't seem to feel at all guilty about it. I see it happen all the time, and afterward I always say to myself, "I should have said something." So finally I did.

I was walking down my block the other day, and this guy was coming toward me, and he threw his cup right into my neighbor's garden! What nerve! Now, I could have ignored it and carried on walking without saying a thing – as I usually do – but I know I would have regretted it. I was determined to do something this time because it was right there in my neighborhood! So I yelled at him. I probably shouldn't have done that, but I kind of lost my temper! I said, "You know, Mrs. Tweedy worked really hard on that garden, and you just threw your trash in it. And there's a garbage can right on the corner!" He seemed pretty embarrassed and said, "You're right. I'm sorry." Then he went and got his cup. I was really surprised, but I'm glad it turned out like that – he could have gotten mad at me or turned aggressive or something. Anyway, I felt great for the rest of the day, and in the future, I'll always stop and tell people to pick up their trash – though I probably won't yell like that!

Evan, 22, Chicago I can't stand it when people I know send me spam! I mean, getting commercial spam is bad enough, but from your friends? I'm talking about those silly jokes and "funny" stories people send you every day. They e-mail everyone in their address book. Half the time, I bet they don't even read those ridiculous stories. They just click "send," and presto – instant junk mail. It's so impersonal! I mean, sometimes I see something funny I want to send to someone, but I always include a personal note. And I don't send things to everybody in my entire address book.

I have this friend who used to send me junk mail all the time – like three or four every day. I finally couldn't take it anymore, and I asked her very nicely to stop. At first, she was insulted and her feelings were hurt. But then she understood. Turns out, someone had started sending her tons of junk mail, too! So I think she finally sympathized with me! And now I can get through my e-mail much more quickly, so it all worked out OK.

B Find these words and phrases in the article. Match them with their definitions.

1. pet peeves ___f___
2. toss _____
3. What nerve! _____
4. carried on _____
5. couldn't take it _____
6. insulted _____

a. continued
b. How rude!
c. couldn't stand it
d. offended
e. throw
f. frustrations; irritations

C **Read the blogs again. Then answer the questions.**

1. What does Margaret usually do when she sees people throw trash on the street? _____
   _____

2. Why did she decide to respond differently this time? _____

3. What does she think she should have done differently? _____

4. Why doesn't Evan like getting spam from his friends? _____

5. Why did Evan's friend finally sympathize with him? _____

2 Apologies

Writing **A** **Read the note of apology. Fill in the blanks with the expressions in the box.**

I feel I should apologize for	I promise not to	I should have	it was my fault entirely

Dear Mr. Feaster,

_____ letting my dog run in your garden the other day. I was talking on my cell phone, and I didn't notice he was digging up your flowers. _____ paid more attention. I know _____ . _____ let my dog into your garden again. I hope you accept my apology.

Sincerely,
Janice Brown

B **Think of something you've done in the past, and write a note of apology.**

Unit 8 Progress chart

Mark the boxes below to rate your progress. ✔ = I know how to . . . ? = I need to review how to . . .	To review, go back to these pages in the Student's Book.
Grammar ☐ use past modals to talk hypothetically about the past	76 and 77
☐ use past modals to speculate about the past	79
Vocabulary ☐ use at least 6 words and expressions to discuss behavior	76 and 77
☐ use 15 new words to talk about emotions and personality	78
Conversation strategies ☐ use expressions like *Speaking of* and *That's like* to share my experiences	80
☐ use *like* in different ways	81
Writing ☐ use expressions to apologize	83

Unit 9 Material world

Possessions

1 Things and stuff

Vocabulary

A Complete the questions with the words and expressions in the box.

accumulated	materialistic	part with
goals	✓ own	possessions

1. Do you ____own____ a lot of valuable things?
2. How attached are you to the things you own – your _____ ?
3. What things do you find hard to throw away or _____ ?
4. What kinds of objects have you collected or _____ over time?
5. What are your main aims or _____ for this coming year?
6. How _____ are you?

B Answer the questions from part A with your own information.

1. _I don't own anything of great value, really, but I want to start collecting art._
   I have a lot of personal items, like clothes and books, though.
2. _____
   _____
3. _____
   _____
4. _____
   _____
5. _____
   _____
6. _____
   _____

2 What did they say?

Grammar and vocabulary

Read the statements. Then complete the sentences to report what the people said.

1. "I think I'll clean out my closets today."
   Melissa said that she <u>thought</u> she <u>'d clean out</u> her closets today.
2. "I've been saving money to buy a new car."
   Josh said that he _____ money to buy a new car.
3. "I haven't found a new dress for Junko's party yet."
   Leah said that she _____ a new dress for Junko's party yet.
4. "I can't part with my favorite jeans, even though they're torn."
   Hong said he _____ his favorite jeans,
   even though they _____ torn.
5. "My goal is to pay off my credit card debt by next year."
   Rupert said that his goal _____ to pay off his credit card
   debt by next year.
6. "I'm always buying CDs. I think I have about 1,000."
   Pedro said that he _____ CDs and that he _____
   he _____ about 1,000.
7. "I won't ever throw out my favorite photographs."
   Julia said that she _____ her favorite photographs.
8. "My parents bought me a beautiful pearl necklace."
   Erin said that her parents _____ her a beautiful pearl necklace.

3 Her mother's a millionaire.

Grammar

Rewrite the direct speech as reported speech.

Mel Did you have a good time on your date with Ariel last week?
I saw her at a café yesterday, and she said ____<u>she had enjoyed it a lot</u>____ .
("I enjoyed it a lot.")

Eric Yeah, it was fine. The only thing was I had to pay for everything.
Ariel said _____ . Then she said
("I'm broke.")
that _____ .
("I've been spending too much lately.")

Mel So you paid for the movies and dinner, too?
Eric Yes. She said _____ .
("I can't afford to buy the tickets.")

Mel Are you going to see her again?
Eric I don't know. She told me _____
("I'm going away for a week.")
and that _____ .
("I'll call you when I get back.")

Mel I hope she doesn't get back before your next paycheck!
Where's she going anyway?
Eric Well, she said _____ .
("It's a surprise.")
Her mother was sending her someplace exotic.
Mel Yeah. She once told me _____ .
("My mother's a millionaire.")

67

1 Money matters

Vocabulary | Circle the correct word to complete each money expression.

1. get into   a. money   (b.) debt   c. payment
2. pay good   a. account   b. budget   c. interest
3. pay in   a. cash   b. check   c. credit card
4. invest   a. account   b. money   c. debt
5. keep track   a. off   b. aside   c. of
6. pay by   a. check   b. stock   c. bills
7. set ___ money   a. away   b. aside   c. off
8. pay ___ a loan   a. off   b. away   c. aside
9. take out   a. an interest   b. a debt   c. a loan

2 Smart money tips

Vocabulary | Complete the sentences and puzzle below with the words in the box.

away	bills	✓charge	debt	income	monthly	out	savings	stocks

1. Don't _charge_ too much to your credit card, unless you can pay it off in full every month.
2. It's important to pay your _____ on time. You shouldn't let them pile up.
3. Sticking to a _____ budget can save you money.
4. Many people take _____ loans to pay for cars or homes.
5. Try to put _____ some money every month for emergencies.
6. Shop around for a _____ account that pays good interest.
7. People sometimes take several jobs to increase their _____ .
8. You can invest in a company by buying _____ .
9. It's important to get out of _____ to avoid paying large sums of interest.

1.   c h a r g e
2.   __ __ __ __ __
3.   __ __ __ __ __ __
4.   __ __ __
5.   __ __ __ __
6.   __ __ __ __ __ __ __
7.   __ __ __ __ __ __
8.   __ __ __ __ __ __
9.   __ __ __ __

When children do chores around the house, they often get an _____ .

3 He asked me . . .

Grammar Imagine you met with a financial advisor to talk about your spending habits.
Read the financial advisor's questions. Then complete the reported questions.

1. "How much money do you save each month?"
   He asked me <u>how much money I saved</u> each month.
2. "Do you have any credit card or other debt?"
   He wanted to know _____ any credit card or other debt.
3. "Can you stick to a monthly budget?"
   He wanted to know _____ a monthly budget.
4. "How many times have you taken money out of your savings account this month?"
   He asked _____ money out of my savings account this month.
5. "What do you spend most of your money on?"
   He wanted to know _____ most of my money on.
6. "Have you taken out a loan recently?"
   He asked me _____ a loan recently.

4 Where did the money go?

Grammar Read what Amy says and the questions her family asks her. Then change the
direct questions into reported questions by completing the sentences below.

Amy's sister asked her . . .

1. <u>whether / if she wanted to borrow some money</u> .
2. _____ .

Amy's father asked her . . .

3. _____ .
4. _____ .

Amy's mother asked her . . .

5. _____ .
6. _____ .

She was telling me . . .

1 What was she telling you?

Read these reports of conversations. Rewrite the underlined sentences as reported speech using past continuous reporting verbs.

I was talking with my neighbor yesterday. (1) She told me about her son. He's planning to do some community work for a few years. (2) She said it doesn't pay much. But he thinks it'll be a good experience anyway.

(3) A co-worker of mine told me our boss just won the lottery. I can't believe it! She never buys lottery tickets! But she bought one on impulse, and she won! (4) My co-worker said she won $5,000. So, hopefully, she might buy us lunch today.

(5) My friend told me she needs a new car. Her car is always breaking down, and she's been late to work five times this month. (6) She said that she might lose her job if she's late again.

I was talking to my brother on the phone last night. (7) I told him what to do while I'm on vacation. So, he's going to feed my cat and water my plants. And I told him where things were.

1. <u>She was telling me about her son.</u>

2. _____
   _____

3. _____
   _____

4. _____
   _____

5. _____
   _____

6. _____
   _____

7. _____
   _____

2 Who told you?

Conversation strategies

Complete the conversations with the expressions in the boxes.

✓evidently	I've heard	told me

1. *A* Wow! We have so much stuff in our closets. There's no more room.
   B I know. <u>Evidently</u> , there's a new TV show where this woman helps you get rid of all the stuff you don't want anymore.
   A Really?
   B Yeah, Seth _____ about it. They take everything you own and put it outside your house. You have to sell or throw away more than half of it!
   A Oh, yeah. _____ it's a fun show.

according to the report	they say	was saying

2. *A* Did you hear the news about interest rates?
   B Yeah, I did. _____ on TV last night, they're going up – again!
   A That's right. _____ we'll have to pay around 25 percent on our credit cards.
   B I know. Isn't that terrible?
   A Yeah. But, as my friend _____ , it might stop us from spending so much.

apparently	he was telling me	I was told

3. *A* Did you get tickets for the school concert tonight?
   B It's tonight? _____ it was next week.
   A No, it's tonight. _____ , it's going to be a great show. I talked to Henry earlier today, and _____ it's already sold out.
   B Oh, no. I guess I'm not going, then.

3 About you

Answer the questions with true information. Use past continuous reporting verbs and expressions from Exercise 2.

1. What's an interesting TV show you've heard about recently?

   _____

2. What's something you learned from the news?

   _____

3. What's some good or bad news someone just told you this week?

   _____

1 *Leaving your books behind*

Reading   **A** **Read the article. What do BookCrossers do with their books?**

☐ give them to a library   ☐ leave them in public places   ☐ sell them on a Web site

The world is your

Library!

When Judy Redding finishes a book, she doesn't put it back on her bookshelf. She "releases" it. Sometimes she leaves it on a park bench, sometimes in a coffee shop, sometimes on a subway train. Redding isn't forgetful, and she's not littering. She is one of more than 400,000 BookCrossers who are members of a Web site that promotes the exchange of books with readers around the world.

According to the site, its goal is "to make the whole world a library." Founder Ron Hornbaker came up with the idea with his wife, Kaori, while admiring a Web site that tracks disposable cameras and publishes the pictures. In April 2001, they launched BookCrossing.com, and since then, the site has become very popular, gaining about 300 new members a day.

The site's motto is "Read, Register, Release," and here's how it works. When you've finished a book, go to the BookCrossing Web site and register it. You will receive an ID number for your book. Then write the ID number inside the book, and label the book with information about the site. Next, take the book out in public and leave it there! If someone finds it and goes to the Web site, they can enter the ID number of the book. The site then sends you an e-mail letting you know that it has been "caught." The site is free to use.

You can write a journal entry on the site about what you thought of the book you released, and the person who finds it can add his or her comments, too. More than 2.4 million books have been registered on the site, yet it's hard to track exactly how many books have actually been found. Redding has released 25 books so far and has received five confirmations that her books have been caught. But it doesn't matter to her because she loves the adventure of sharing books that she likes. If someone finds it and becomes a BookCrosser, all the better.

B **Read the article again. Write *T* (true) or *F* (false) for each sentence. Then correct the false sentences.**

1. BookCrossers, like Judy Redding, always leave their books in ~~the same place.~~ *different places* __F__
2. BookCrossing.com's goal is to create a kind of worldwide library. ____
3. Before you leave a book in public, you put a label with information about the book inside it. ____
4. You have to pay to use BookCrossing.com. ____
5. People can write journal entries on the Web site about the books they've read. ____
6. Redding has tracked all the books that she has released. ____

2 *So many books*

Writing **A** Read the article about a book lover. Fill in the blanks with the expressions in the box.

she added	she concluded	✓ she explained	she recalled

Eunjoo Park has more than 5,000 books in her one-bedroom apartment. "I can't live without my books," she explained . Her living room and bedroom are filled with bookshelves, and she is always buying more shelves. "It's better to buy more shelves than get rid of any books," _____ .

"Once, I decided to sell some books in a street sale," _____ . "When a woman came by and tried to buy a book, I couldn't sell it to her! I took my books back inside and put them away."

Now she knows better. "I just refuse to get rid of my books," she told me. "There seems to be only one solution – I just have to get a bigger apartment," _____ .

B Write an article about someone you know. Use reporting verbs to tell the person's story. Use an idea below or one of your own.

Someone who . . .
• collects something.
• often sells his or her things.
• is materialistic.

_____
_____
_____
_____
_____
_____

Unit 9 Progress chart

Mark the boxes below to rate your progress. ☑ = I know how to . . . ? = I need to review how to . . .	To review, go back to these pages in the Student's Book.
Grammar ☐ report what someone said ☐ report what someone asked	86 and 87 89
Vocabulary ☐ use 25 new expressions about possessions and money	86, 87, 88, and 89
Conversation strategies ☐ use past continuous reporting verbs to tell about a conversation ☐ use expressions like *They say*, *I've heard*, and *Evidently*	90 91
Writing ☐ use different reporting verbs to quote other people	93

Unit 10 Fame

The rise to fame

1 Kelly Clarkson's rise to fame

Grammar Read the information about pop star Kelly Clarkson. Then complete the sentences below using the past perfect and past modals.

Kelly Clarkson was chosen from among hundreds of competitors to win *American Idol*, a TV talent show that lets viewers vote on the winner. Since winning in 2002, she has recorded a number of top-selling "hits" and has become a household name. Yet, her rise to fame came somewhat unexpectedly, as she had always dreamed of being a marine biologist.

1. If Kelly _had followed_ (follow) her career dream, she _might have become_ (might become) a marine biologist.
2. If a music teacher _____ (not hear) Kelly singing in the hall of her middle school, she _____ (not join) the school chorus.
3. If Kelly _____ (not learn) to sing classically in her school chorus, she _____ (might not be able) to use her voice in so many different ways.
4. If Kelly's friend _____ (not tell) her about *American Idol*, Kelly _____ (not try out) for the show.
5. If Kelly _____ (receive) 47% and not 57% of the final vote on *American Idol*, she _____ (not win) the competition.

2 More pop idols

Grammar Complete the interviews with the runners-up of a TV talent competition with the past perfect or past modal form of the verbs given. Sometimes more than one answer is possible.

A POP MAGAZINE EXCLUSIVE The Pop Artists You Voted For!

The Runners-Up

Beth Simon

PM   Why do you think you came in second, Beth?
Beth   I definitely chose the wrong song. The judges didn't like it at all.
PM   So, if you _____ (not sing) that song, _____ you _____ (win), do you think?
Beth   Who knows? I _____ (have) a better chance. But it doesn't really matter because I had a great time.

Ian Wong

PM   How are you feeling, Ian?
Ian   Well, I didn't realize how hard it would be. If I _____ (know), maybe I _____ (work) harder on my singing.
PM   _____ you _____ (take) more singing lessons?
Ian   Yeah, I _____ (look) for a voice teacher and maybe a dance teacher, too!

3 *She might have become a famous ballerina.*

Grammar | **Complete each story with your own ideas. Use past modals.**

1. Emma was a top student in high school and in her dance classes. But then she dropped out of dance class to focus on her schoolwork. She then went on to study at Harvard University. If Emma hadn't stopped taking dance classes, <u>she might have / could have become a famous ballerina</u> **or** <u>she wouldn't have gone to Harvard</u>.

2. Maemi always wanted to be a doctor, but on her 13th birthday, her parents gave her a camera. That was the start of her interest in photography, and she later became a professional photographer. If Maemi hadn't gotten a camera for her birthday, _____ .

3. Stephanie loved to build things when she was younger. She even helped her father design an addition to their house. But when she was in high school, she was spotted by a modeling agency and became a model. She always says that _____ if she hadn't become a model.

4. Martin loved farming, but he had no interest in cooking. His grandmother nevertheless made him help her cook dinner every Sunday. Martin just opened his second organic restaurant. If his grandmother hadn't taught him how to cook, _____ .

5. Hao-xing, a trombone player, was taking part in a competition. As he stepped on stage, he noticed a beautiful woman in the front row of the audience. While he was playing his piece, he became distracted by the woman. He forgot the music and didn't win the competition. If he hadn't seen the woman, _____ .

4 *About you*

Grammar | **Complete the sentences with past modals and your own ideas.**

1. If I had left school at the age of 16, <u>I might not have met the teacher who inspired me the most</u> .
2. If I hadn't taken English, _____ .
3. _____ if I hadn't worked so hard.
4. If I had been born into a famous family, _____ .
5. _____ if I had practiced more.
6. If my parents hadn't _____ , _____ .

In the public eye

1 Making headlines

Vocabulary Complete the magazine article with the expressions in the box.

bad press	in the headlines
drop out of sight	in the right place
go downhill	made headlines
got discovered	take off
have connections	✓up-and-coming

Lucky Star

 Up-and-coming movie star Gianna LaRose was seen having lunch with her boyfriend of two years, Rich Marsh, in Los Angeles earlier this week. The couple seemed relaxed and happy, even after the _____ their relationship has gotten recently. Ms. LaRose denied rumors of a split and happily signed autographs for her fans.

 After losing last year's Best Breakthrough Performance Award, many people thought LaRose's career could only _____, but just the opposite has happened. Ms. LaRose _____ recently when she was offered the lead role in director Rick Callahan's new blockbuster. This young actress has everything going for her. It's unlikely she will _____ anytime soon. Her career is just getting started and is sure to _____ .

 Ms. LaRose _____ five years ago while working at a movie theater. Talent agent Erica Menken saw LaRose and thought she had "star qualities." The rest is history, as they say. Ms. LaRose says she was lucky to meet Ms. Menken. She was studying to be an actress, but she didn't _____ in the movie industry. "Meeting Erica was an example of being _____ at the right time," Ms. LaRose said.

 Expect to see Ms. LaRose's name _____ for a long time.

2 A movie date

Grammar Complete the sentences below with the tag questions in the box.

1. It's great to go out and see a movie, ___isn't it___ ?

2. We're not going to be late for the movie, _____ ?

3. You haven't seen this movie yet, _____ ?

4. You liked the movie, _____ ?

5. It was interesting, _____ ?

6. That actor has been in a lot of films, _____ ?

are we
didn't you
hasn't he
have you
✓isn't it
wasn't it

3 Stars among us

Grammar **Complete the conversations with the tag questions.**

1. **A** Ben Affleck gives a lot of money to charity, <u>doesn't he</u> ?

   B I didn't know that. You don't see it in the press very much, _____ ?

   A No, but then, people often do charitable things quietly, _____ ?

   B Maybe. But it's great to see someone who's so wealthy give money to good causes, _____ ?

   A Sure, but I wish someone would give some to me!

2. **A** Oh, my goodness. That isn't Sheryl Crow, _____ ?

   B I don't think so. She doesn't go shopping in this mall, _____ ?

   A I don't know. I think it's her. She just signed that girl's shirt, _____ ?

   B Hmm. It does kind of look like her, _____ ?

   A See, I was right, _____ ? Come on. Let's go over and get her autograph, too!

4 Tell us about yourself.

Grammar **Imagine you are going to interview actor Reese Witherspoon. Write tag questions you can ask her to check the following facts.**

Facts	Questions
1. raised in Nashville, Tennessee	You were raised in Tennessee, weren't you?
2. started acting at the age of seven	
3. first major role was in The Man in the Moon	
4. appeared in over 25 movies by the age of 30	
5. has produced several films	
6. married to actor Ryan Phillippe	
7. has two children	

Good question!

1 Comic advice

Complete the conversation with tag questions.

Tina Hey, Max. How was the comedy workshop you went to last week?

Max Great. I'd like to be a comedian someday, but I'm not sure I'm ready.

Tina Well, you could take another comedy workshop, _couldn't you_ ?

Max Yeah. . . . There's another one next month.

Tina Sounds good. You just need to call and sign up, _____ ?

Max Yeah. I wonder how all the famous comedians on TV got started.

Tina It would help to read some books about them, _____ ?

Max I guess. I'll go to the bookstore tonight. You know, the hardest thing is writing new and original jokes.

Tina Well, you could look for some books on joke writing, too, _____ ?

Max Yeah. I mean, I learned a bit about it in the workshop, but you never can tell what people will find funny.

Tina It would be a good idea to call some of the local comedy clubs, _____ ? And ask them if you could try out some of your jokes. They always need people to perform, _____ ? I'm sure the club owners could give you some advice, too. I mean, you need all the help you can get, _____ ?

Max Hey, that's not funny!

2 What's your advice?

Your friend is having a lot of bad luck lately. Read each situation and give your best advice and encouragement using tag questions.

1. I didn't do well on the last English test. I'm worried about my final grade.
   I'm sure you could ask to take the test again, couldn't you?

2. I want to practice my English, but I don't know any English-speaking people.
   _____

3. I got in a horrible fight with my best friend. I don't know what to do.
   _____

4. I've gained some weight over the holidays. I don't fit into my jeans!
   _____

5. I forgot my boyfriend's birthday and never got him a present.
   _____

6. I lost my mother's necklace. What am I going to do?
   _____

3 That's a good question.

Conversation strategies

Match each question with the best response.

1. What's the hardest thing about being famous? __b__
2. What do you plan to do next in your career? _____
3. Who inspires you in your work? _____
4. Do you consider yourself a role model? _____
5. What would you do if you weren't an actor? _____

a. That's a good question. I think I'd like to do some roles in theater.
b. That's a tough one. I'd say it's probably always being in the public eye. You have no privacy.
c. Good question. Actually, I can't imagine doing anything else, really.
d. It's hard to say. There are so many good actors. I admire a lot of them.
e. Oh, definitely. I try to set a good example for young people.

4 To be famous or not to be famous . . .

Conversation strategies

Number the lines of the conversation in the correct order.

_____ But if you were famous, you would be hanging out with other famous people, wouldn't you? That sounds like fun to me!

_____ It's hard to say. Even if you're famous, you might not make a lot of money. Some politicians are famous, but they aren't rich – and they don't wear expensive clothes!

__1__ You want to be an actor, right? You *would* like to be famous someday, wouldn't you?

_____ I'm not saying that wouldn't be fun. I just kind of like my privacy, that's all.

_____ Oh, that's a tough question. Being famous would be nice, but I don't know if I'd like all the stuff that goes with it. I like acting. But that doesn't mean I want to be famous!

_____ I know what you mean, but just think, you'd make a lot of money. Then you could buy all kinds of cool clothes, couldn't you?

Pulling through

1 Rap image

Reading

A Read the article. Why do you think rap stars maintain their "bad boy" image?

Jay-Z   Missy Elliott

Many celebrities seem to be at ease with their fame, as if they had been born in the public eye. We see them in movies, on TV, and on magazine covers, shining back at us with perfect skin, hair, and clothes. It seems as though these celebrities have always been rich and famous, and it's hard to imagine their lives ever being any different. However, there is one notable group of stars that got their start on city streets where life was never easy, perfect, or glamorous.

Rap music started in the 1970s in a poor part of New York City, where life was often difficult and dangerous because of crime, unemployment, drugs, and violence. At that time, rappers like Grandmaster Flash and the Furious Five created rap as a form of poetry that reflected the way people like themselves lived in such a hard, inner-city neighborhood. Soon, hanging out with friends and rapping – and listening to others rap – became a way for many teenagers living on such tough city streets to express themselves creatively. Rap quickly spread to other cities in the United States and then became a worldwide phenomenon.

Even after its global success, many rap stars – such as 50 Cent, Jay-Z, Nelly, Missy Elliott, and Eminem – still come from poor or violent urban neighborhoods. Moreover, as rap artists become rich and famous, many choose to keep their tough "street image." For example, their songs continue to reflect the language of the underprivileged neighborhoods where they grew up, and their clothes and accessories reflect – and influence – the style of urban youth around the world. However, some music fans are uncomfortable with the "bad boy" image of rap, especially with gangsta rappers, whom they criticize for including violent lyrics in their songs.

Rap is now part of a larger cultural phenomenon known as hip-hop, which has become a very successful and profitable industry. Hip-hop has inspired movies like *8 Mile* and influenced fashion design such as Rocawear and Sean John. Despite the billions of dollars the hip-hop industry has made through music, film, and fashion, it continues to maintain its tough street image – reflecting the environment that created it.

B Read the article again. Write *T* (true) or *F* (false). Then correct the false statements.

1. Rap started in a ~~wealthy~~ (poor) neighborhood in New York City in the 1970s. __F__

2. Rap was a way for kids in bad neighborhoods to get into trouble. _____

3. After rap became popular, many of its stars came from rich backgrounds. _____

4. Eminem came from a privileged background. _____

5. Many rap stars don't like their controversial image. _____

6. Rap music is often criticized for its violence. _____

7. Rap and hip-hop have inspired movies and clothing. _____

2 *A controversial rap star*

Writing **A** Read the paragraph about Eminem. Underline the topic sentence. Then cross out any information that does not support the topic.

Eminem is one of the most popular and controversial rap stars of the decade. He is known for his distinctive style of changing his pace several times within a song without losing the beat. He often uses a lot of bad language in his songs. He has been married and has one daughter. He is also famous for telling stories in his songs, talking about his own life and childhood, making fun of celebrities, and criticizing politicians. He has short blond hair and often wears baggy jeans and sweatshirts. Unlike most rap stars who come from New York and Los Angeles, Eminem is from Detroit.

B Write a paragraph about a famous person. Write a strong topic sentence, and add more information and details in supporting sentences.

Unit 10 Progress chart

Mark the boxes below to rate your progress. ☑ = I know how to . . . ? = I need to review how to . . .	To review, go back to these pages in the Student's Book.
Grammar ☐ talk hypothetically about the past using *if* clauses with the past perfect form of the verb and past modals	98 and 99
☐ use negative and affirmative tag questions	100 and 101
Vocabulary ☐ use at least 8 idiomatic expressions to talk about fame	98, 99, 100, and 101
Conversation strategies ☐ soften advice and give encouragement using tag questions	102
☐ use expressions like *That's a tough one* when questions are difficult to answer	103
Writing ☐ write a paragraph with a topic sentence and supporting sentences	105

Unit 11 Trends

Trends in society

1 On the Web

Vocabulary Complete the news stories with the words in the box.

financial support	outsource	shortage	unemployment
obsessed	recruit	traffic congestion	✓wireless Internet access

---

Search
The Internet Search Engine

Images Groups News Local More>>

Search

Web   Results of **1-100** of about **969,000** for **Washingtonville** *(0.30 seconds)*

RESULTS FOR CURRENT TOP NEWS STORIES: LOCAL: Washingtonville

Technology news

Local coffee shop to offer __wireless Internet access__ . Owner says it's necessary to compete with the large coffee shop chains.

Business

Several companies have announced they will _____ their customer service jobs and lay off staff. Local _____ rates are expected to jump three percent.

Increased demand for the latest hybrid cars has created a _____ at local car dealers.

Local companies are expecting to _____ over 600 employees at the annual job fair this year.

Health

Is our culture _____ with dieting and being thin? Dr. Murphy examines the diet craze and the new "designer" diets.

Education

Tuition fees at colleges across the country are rising at an alarming rate. Local financial expert Ken Rose explains what kind of _____ is available.

Local traffic

_____ is expected in the Washingtonville Bridge area again tomorrow. Delays are due to the ongoing bridge repairs.

---

2 Current trends

 **Grammar** Complete the sentences with the passive form of the present continuous or present perfect.

1. Technology companies are designing smaller and smaller musical devices. Some devices, as small as a credit card, <u>are being sold</u> (sell) in stores around the country right now.

2. Automakers have manufactured a new kind of vehicle. Hybrid cars that use a combination of gas and electricity _____ (develop) to lower gas consumption.

3. Scientists are exploring ways to make plants like wheat, corn, and tomatoes disease-resistant. These plants _____ (engineer) and tested on farms around the world.

4. Sports clothing companies are trying to incorporate technology into their clothing. Currently, vests, shirts, and pants _____ (create) to help athletes improve their performance by measuring muscle activity.

5. Many companies have now outsourced information technology jobs. These jobs _____ (move) overseas to cut company costs.

6. Research has shown that children in the United States are gaining weight. Several studies _____ (conduct) by researchers and show that 16 percent of U.S. children are overweight.

3 In the news

Grammar Write sentences about the headlines using the verbs given. Use the passive form of the present continuous or the present perfect. Sometimes more than one answer is possible.

> **At last, a cure for the common cold**

1. (find) <u>At last, a cure for the common cold has been found.</u>

> **The world's oldest building in Japan**

2. (discover) _____

> **New driving tests for next year**

3. (schedule) _____

> **Traffic slow because of strong storms**

4. (delay) _____

> **Plans to hire more teachers**

5. (discuss) _____

Environmental matters

1 An environmental puzzle

Vocabulary | **Complete the sentences. Then unscramble the highlighted letters to complete the sentence below.**

1. Due to the lack of rain, we are experiencing a d r o u g h t .

2. Garbage that isn't recycled ends up in a ___ ___ ___ ___ ___ ___ ___ .

3. Scientists think that polar ice caps are melting at an ever-increasing rate because of
   ___ ___ ___ ___ ___ ___   ___ ___ ___ ___ ___ ___ ___ .

4. Many fish are dying because of the ___ ___ ___ ___ ___
   ___ ___ ___ ___ ___ ___ ___ ___ ___ that factories dump into rivers every day.

5. If we continue to use our ___ ___ ___ ___ ___ ___ ___
   ___ ___ ___ ___ ___ ___ ___ ___ , like oil and coal, they might run out.

6. Scientists have been working on ___ ___ ___ ___ ___ ___ ___ ___ ___ ___ ___ –
   ___ ___ ___ ___ ___ ___ ___ ___ transportation, like hybrid cars, to cut down on pollution.

7. Some man-made materials are not ___ ___ ___ ___ ___ ___ ___ ___ ___ ___ ___ ___ .
   They can take years to break down.

8. I want a car that ___ ___ ___ ___ ___ ___ ___ ___ less gas because gas prices are rising!

_____ energy by turning off lights when you leave home.

2 Conservation tips

Vocabulary | **Circle the correct words to complete the sentences. Then check (✓) the things you do to help.**

1. ___ Use **biodegradable** / (**energy-saving**) / **renewable energy** home appliances to
   cut back on electricity use.

2. ___ Avoid using plastic containers that take years to **consume** / **recycle** /
   decompose in landfill sites.

3. ___ Encourage government officials to pass tougher laws to reduce
   air pollution / **public transportation** / **endangered species**.

4. ___ Take shorter showers and remember to turn off the faucet while you brush
   your teeth to reduce **nuclear waste** / **water consumption** / **water pollution**.

5. ___ Try to **recycle** / **consume** / **use** plastic, paper, and glass if possible.

6. ___ Buy appliances like refrigerators and air conditioners that **lack** /
   decompose / **consume** lower amounts of energy.

7. ___ Be aware of companies that **protect** / **contaminate** / **dispose of** rivers with
   toxic chemicals, and don't buy their products.

8. ___ If you think you **buy** / **take** / **lack** information on ways to save energy or
   conserve water, search the Internet for ideas.

3 *Environmental awareness*

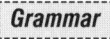

Grammar | Circle the word or expression that best fits each sentence.

1. I think the majority of people would prefer to buy organic produce **due to** / (**despite**) the high cost.

2. We always turn our heat down a few degrees in the winter **in order to** / **instead of** save money on oil.

3. Gas prices have gone up **due to** / **although** oil shortages.

4. We try to recycle plastic, paper, and glass, **although** / **so that** it's sometimes hard to do.

5. We're experiencing more hurricanes and severe storms **as a result of** / **because** global warming.

6. I think some people aren't very aware of environmental problems **instead of** / **because of** a lack of education.

4 *It's important because . . .*

Grammar | Complete the sentences with the words and expressions in the box.

✓because	due to	in order to	in spite of	instead of	so that

1. It's important to keep the world's oceans and seas free of pollution and contamination **because** we depend on these waters for food.

2. Car companies are beginning to make some cars out of lightweight carbon fiber instead of steel _____ increase gas mileage.

3. Governments need to work together _____ endangered species are protected around the world.

4. The Amazon rain forest is being deforested twice as quickly as previously thought _____ logging activities.

5. Governments should invest in renewable energy _____ the cost.

6. Some people use vegetable oil to run their cars _____ gasoline.

5 *About you*

Grammar and Vocabulary | Complete the sentences with true information. Use linking words and expressions.

1. I try to use **less electricity in order to save money each month** _____ .

2. I try not to waste _____ .

3. I always buy _____ .

4. I'm concerned about _____ .

5. I think governments should _____ .

Like I said, . . .

1 Referring back

Conversation strategies

A Taya and Yasuo are talking about current trends. Match Taya's comments with Yasuo's comments later in the conversation.

1. A lot of big companies are employing workers like telephone operators overseas because it's cheaper. I'm not sure that's fair. _e_

2. I think we have some of the longest working hours in the world in this country. It's awful. ____

3. The cost of health care is getting higher and higher. It's not right that so many people can't afford health insurance. ____

4. I think it's great that people can work more from home now. It's much better for family life. ____

5. I heard they're increasing the retirement age to 70! I mean, do you think people should work that long? ____

a. Like you were saying, not commuting every day can only be good for everyone, especially people with kids.

b. As you said, it's not right that so many people can't afford medical care when they need it.

c. Going back to what you were saying about raising the retirement age, I actually think it's a good idea.

d. Like you said earlier, it's not healthy that we work so much overtime. How do people spend time with their families?

e. You mentioned transferring jobs abroad earlier. I agree that it's not good for local workers.

B Look at Taya's comments in part A again. Refer back to each comment she makes, and add your own view.

1. As Taya was saying, I don't think big companies should move jobs overseas. I mean, what will people do here to earn money?

2. _____

3. _____

4. _____

5. _____

2 And so on and so forth . . .

 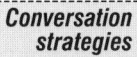 **Complete the conversations with the phrases in the box and a more formal vague expression like *and so forth, and so on,* or *etc.***

> ✓chemical engineers, electrical engineers,
>   more on-the-job experience, good leadership qualities,
>   organizational skills, good people skills,
>
> paid leave, flexible work hours,
> relax, reduce stress, pursue interests,
> vision care, dental care,

1. *A* I think engineering is a great field for students to study. It offers some of the best-paid jobs for students just graduating from college.
   B Yes. Some of the highest starting salaries go to <u>chemical engineers, electrical</u> <u>engineers, etc.</u>

2. *A* It's too bad that some companies are cutting back on medical benefits.
   B Yeah, I know. My company has cut things like _____ _____ .

3. *A* I don't think it's fair that companies are encouraging older workers to retire because they make more money than younger workers.
   B I totally agree. Older workers have _____ _____ .

4. *A* I'm thinking about starting a family, but I'm really nervous about trying to work and raise a child at the same time.
   B I wouldn't worry. Lots of companies offer new parents benefits like _____ _____ .

5. *A* I think when you're hiring a new employee, you need someone with a good personality. I think personality is the most important thing.
   B I agree, but I also think you should look for someone with _____ _____ .

6. *A* I think all workers should have at least four weeks of paid vacation a year.
   B Absolutely. I mean, vacations allow people to _____ _____ .

3 About you

  **Imagine you heard these comments in a conversation. Refer back to them, and give your view. Use a formal vague expession.**

1. "There should be fines for people who don't recycle."
   <u>As you said, fines would make people recycle, make money to improve recycling</u> <u>programs, and so on.</u>

2. "Global warming is really impacting our climate."
   _____

3. "People should use public transportation."
   _____

Technological change

1 Trendy words

Reading **A** Match the terms and definitions. Read the article to check your answers.

1. ego-surfers __e__
2. cyberslackers ___
3. phishers ___
4. wiki ___
5. screenagers ___
6. netizens ___

a. a Web page that anyone can add to and / or change
b. people who attempt to steal other people's identities
c. people who go on the Internet for their personal use at work
d. people who are confident with technology
e. people who look themselves up on the Internet
f. young people who spend a lot of time on the computer

In erne Vocabulary

Whether you embrace technological change or not, getting news and entertainment from the Internet is here to stay. And along with it comes the creation of new words to describe the uses and users of these new technologies. A quick look at the most current dictionaries shows an avalanche of new words entering our language at a record pace. Here are some of them.

ego-surfer An ego-surfer looks for mentions of himself or herself on the Internet by using search engines. Some people ego-surf for entertainment. They want to see where their name pops up and what kind of surprising information goes along with it.

cyberslacker A cyberslacker uses his or her company's Internet connection to surf the Web on company time. A cyberslacker might shop, visit a friend's home page, or play games instead of working.

phishing Phishing describes the Internet crime of trying to get someone's personal information (bank account numbers, national identification numbers, etc.) by sending official-looking e-mails and directing unsuspecting victims to fake Web sites. When the user supplies the updated information to these fake Web sites, the phisher uses the information for his or her own purposes.

wiki A Web site where users can add or modify text is called a "wiki." Wikis differ from blogs in that any user can visit a wiki page to search for or update information, making it a continuous work in progress.

screenager This word describes teenagers who are frequently online. A combination of *screen* and *teenager*, a screenager refers to tech-savvy young people raised on computers and TV.

netizen Derived from *citizen*, a netizen is a skilled Internet user. Unlike a newbie, someone who is new to the Internet, a netizen can easily make his or her way around Web sites, finding information quickly.

B Find the words and expressions in the article. Circle the correct meaning.

1. embrace   (a.) welcome   b. understand   c. hate
2. avalanche   a. drop   b. decrease   c. large number
3. pace   a. speed   b. amount   c. cost
4. unsuspecting   a. forgetful   b. trusting   c. young
5. modify   a. remove   b. look up   c. change
6. derived from   a. the same as   b. taken from   c. unlike

2 Trend watch

Writing **A** Use the words and expressions in the box to complete the blog entry.

declined	fewer	growing	increasingly	less	✓more and more

○○○　　　　　　　　　　　　　　　　　　　**Blog**

Have you noticed that <u>more and more</u> people have camera phones? Everywhere I go, I see people taking pictures of each other with their phones. I saw some teens at the mall yesterday taking photos, and they said they were going to download the pictures to their Web sites. I wonder if the sales of regular cameras have _____ due to camera phones. I bet _____ people are using regular cameras these days.

Some people don't even have land phone lines anymore because cell phones are becoming _____ affordable. I mean, they're much _____ expensive than they used to be. Also, the number of cool features available is _____ . You can write an e-mail, get movie times, and even watch the news. In one small device, you have everything you need to stay in touch with the world. It's amazing.

B Write a blog about a trend you've noticed in your town or city. Use words and expressions from part A.

○○○　　　　　　　　　　　　　　　　　　　**Blog**

Unit 11 Progress chart

Mark the boxes below to rate your progress. ☑ = I know how to . . .　　? = I need to review how to . . .	To review, go back to these pages in the Student's Book.
Grammar　☐ use the passive of the present continuous and present perfect	108 and 109
☐ link ideas with expressions like *although*, *due to*, and *so that*	110 and 111
Vocabulary　☐ use at least 8 new expressions to describe trends in society	108 and 109
☐ use at least 15 new expressions to discuss the environment	110 and 111
Conversation strategies　☐ refer back to what someone said with expressions like *As you were saying*, *Like you said*, etc.	112
☐ use formal vague expressions like *and so forth* and *etc.*	113
Writing　☐ use expressions like *more and more* and *increasingly* to describe trends	115

Unit 12 Careers

Finding a career

1 Words for job success

Vocabulary | **Complete the definitions.**

1. The document that lists your educational history and work experience is your _____ résumé _____ .

2. If you work for a company for a short time to get some work experience, it's called an _____ .

3. Someone who can give you guidance and help you choose the right job is a _____ _____ .

4. A meeting where you are asked about your qualifications by a potential employer is an _____ .

5. The things you are good at are your _____ , and the things you are not good at are your _____ .

6. A questionnaire that helps you see what kind of person you are is a _____ .

2 What you need to do is take my advice!

Grammar | **Fern is having some problems at work. Read her concerns and then use the cues to give her advice. Use *What* clauses.**

1. *Fern* I don't feel my boss notices me. I wonder how I can make her see that I'm ready to take on more responsibility and get promoted.

   You What you need is a positive attitude.
   (You need a positive attitude.)

   You _____
   (My friend did something really smart. She wrote a letter to her boss.)

2. *Fern* I've been working here for over a year. How can I ask my boss for a raise?

   You _____
   (I would just ask.)

   You _____
   (You need to get another job offer and then ask for a promotion.)

3. *Fern* I don't think my colleagues take me seriously. How do I get more respect?

   You _____
   (You should wear formal business clothes.)

   You _____
   (You need to get additional skills.)

3 The job market

 **Grammar** | Rewrite the advice below starting with the long noun phrase given.

1. Try and get a really good degree.

   The first thing to do _is to try and get a really good degree_ .

2. Get some work experience in a big company.

   One good thing to get _____ .

3. Be determined to succeed.

   The main thing you need to be _____ .

4. Companies are hiring new graduates right now.

   The good news _____ .

5. Work on improving your English.

   The best thing to do _____ .

6. Internships help you get better jobs.

   The good thing about internships _____ .

4 Online advice

Grammar | Write two answers for the job seekers' online message board. Start one with a *What* clause and another with a long noun phrase.

```
○○○                          Message Board                          ⊖

Threads in forum: Job-seeking advice                                ▲

Question: I had planned to work for a law office during my summer break, but they just told me that
they don't need me. I need a summer job fast! What can I do?
Answer: 1.  What I would do is ask your friends and family members if they
            have any temporary jobs available in their companies.

        2.  _____
            _____

Question: I would love to work at a ski resort for the winter. Does anyone have ideas about what I
could do, and how I can get a job?
Answer: 3.  _____
            _____

        4.  _____
            _____

Question: I don't know what I want to do with my life. Any suggestions for a recent college graduate
who hates to get up in the morning?
Answer: 5.  _____
            _____

        6.  _____
            _____    ▼
```

The world of work

1 Job scramble

Vocabulary Unscramble the jobs. Match them to the areas of work they belong to.

A = Construction industry   *C* = Media and communications
B = Financial services   *D* = Medicine and health care

1. redtio _____editor_____ _C_
2. ronsuge _____ ____
3. cobtreskrok _____ ____
4. trotornacc _____ ____
5. triwer _____ ____
6. raincatdipei _____ ____

7. xat sadrivo _____ ____
8. crustnoontic krerow _____ ____
9. patychirsic suren _____ ____
10. treeprinter _____ ____
11. nailfinca saynalt _____ ____
12. starnatrol _____ ____

2 What jobs are you suited for?

Vocabulary Read what each person says about himself or herself. Write one area of work that each person is suited for and one area of work that each person isn't suited for.

advertising	✓finance	public relations	the travel industry
business management	journalism	publishing	
the construction industry	✓medicine	telemarketing	

1. My parents wanted me to be a doctor, but I can't stand the sight of blood. What I enjoy most is anything to do with money, like banking and investments.

   Suited for: _____finance_____   Not suited for: _____medicine_____

2. I love words, and I'm a pretty good writer. My friends often ask me to look over their papers for mistakes, and I enjoy that. I don't want a job with too much responsibility, like being involved in the planning or organization of a company.

   Suited for: _____   Not suited for: _____

3. I really enjoy building things. In fact, I helped my dad design and build a barn for our farm last year. I'm not really good at things like reading and writing. I'm more practical. Like, I can't imagine writing articles for a newspaper, for example.

   Suited for: _____   Not suited for: _____

4. I'm very sociable and love going to parties and events. I really like meeting people, and I think I'm a good communicator – I get along well with everyone. I would hate being in an office all day and talking to people on the phone.

   Suited for: _____   Not suited for: _____

5. I'm a bit of a homebody, so I don't want a job that takes me away from home a lot. One thing that interests me is how companies promote their products to consumers.

   Suited for: _____   Not suited for: _____

3 *What's in your future?*

Complete the conversations with the future continuous or the future perfect. Sometimes you can use *may* (*not*) and *might* (*not*) instead of *will* or *won't*.

1. **Sasha** I have no idea what I want to do when I graduate from college next year. I really need to make a decision soon!

   Tia Oh, two years from now, you _might / will be running_ (run) your own business.

   Sasha No, I _____ probably _____ (look) for a job that pays more than $7 an hour. But hopefully, I _____ (not ask) you to lend me money!

   Tia That'll be great! But seriously, two years from now, you _____ (finish) your degree, and you _____ (work) on Wall Street.

   Sasha Hmm . . . maybe, or I _____ (live) on a Caribbean island and _____ (work) on the beach.

2. **Malik** I can't believe another year has gone by already.

   Jamie I know. It goes by so fast. I wonder what we _____ (do) this time next year.

   Malik Oh, I don't know. We _____ (live) someplace else, and we _____ (take) a luxury vacation!

   Jamie Yeah, right. We _____ (not pay off) our debts by then, and we still _____ (not fix up) this house, and . . .

   Malik Oh, I hope we _____ (finish) it all by then.

4 *About you*

Answer the questions. Use the future continuous and future perfect.

1. What do you think your life will be like ten years from now?
   I think I'll be working in another country and making a lot of money!

2. Will you still be taking English classes?
   _____

3. What job do you think you'll be doing?
   _____

4. Do you think you'll have changed jobs more than once?
   _____

5. Where will you be living?
   _____

6. Do you think you'll have gotten married or had children?
   _____

1 *The reason I ask is . . .*

Conversation strategies

Complete the conversations with the noun phrases and *What* clauses in the box.

the best thing was (that)	what I heard was (that)
✓the reason I ask is (that)	what I thought was good was (that)
the worst part was (that)	what I was going to tell you was (that)

1. *Jamal* Didn't you once get a job on a farm in Australia?

    Ryan Yeah, I did. Why?

    Jamal Well, <u>the reason I ask is</u> I was wondering whether I should try that myself.

    Ryan You know, I picked garlic. It was hard work, and _____ I smelled of garlic every day. I had to take a long shower at the end of the day to get rid of the garlic smell.

    Jamal Hmm. I think I'd prefer to work on a fruit farm.

2. *Ming-li* Did you hear that the department store at the mall is hiring?

    Thalia No, I didn't. Do you know what positions they're hiring for?

    Ming-li Well, _____ they're hiring temporary sales help for the holiday season. I think the jobs last through the middle of January.

    Thalia Sounds good. I'd love to make a little extra money during the school break. I'll check it out next week.

    Ming-li You should probably go sooner than next week. _____ the store is only hiring about 10 people.

    Thalia Ooh. You're right. I'll go today!

3. *Tomo* What did you think about the job interview we had with Andy Fowler?

    Celia Well, it was OK. I don't know if he's the perfect fit for the company. _____ he had some really interesting ideas about promoting our products. I think he'd be successful in our advertising department.

    Tomo Yeah, he seemed good. He had great qualifications and _____ he has a positive attitude. He doesn't have much solid experience, though.

    Celia Well, you need to be hired to get experience. Maybe we should give him a chance.

2 I don't know if you saw . . .

Conversation
strategies

Read the advertisements. Write sentences about the advertisements with
I don't know if . . . and the cues.

> **Wanted: Energetic, friendly waiters and waitresses to work evenings. Call
> Sergio at the Cactus Bistro for an interview at 888-555-9609.**

1. (see / hire) *I don't know if you've seen the advertisement, but they're hiring*
   waiters and waitresses at the Cactus Bistro.

> *Interested in a new job? Visit the Johnstown Technical College job fair this weekend. Local
> companies are looking for graduates in business management and information technology.*

2. (look for / have) _____

_____

> **Need help writing or revising your résumé? Get creative writing ideas
> from Résumé Express. Call us today at 888-555-4265.**

3. (think about rewriting / get help) _____

_____

> **Announcement:** *Lakewood University is now offering a business
> management degree with an emphasis in advertising and public relations.
> We are currently taking applications for the fall semester.*

4. (hear / get a degree) _____

_____

3 I need some help.

Conversation
strategies

Number the lines of the conversation in the correct order.

_____ Maybe you should get some advice somewhere. I don't know if you're
familiar with the Job Resource Center, but they can give you tips on how to
interview better.

_____ Really? I didn't know you had help finding your job.

_____ I think I *have* heard of it. Is it on Maple Street, near the park?

_____ Oh, yeah. I never would have gotten the job I have right now without their
help. The best part was that they gave me a lot of help with things like
writing my résumé and improving my interview skills.

__1__ I've interviewed for six jobs in the past couple of weeks, and I still haven't
been hired. I really need some help.

_____ Well, I really need to get a job soon, so I'd better check out the Job Resource
Center today!

_____ Yeah, it is. When I was looking for a job last year, I met with a career
counselor there.

1 Important considerations

Reading **A** Read the article. Then add the correct heading to each section.

The Evening Shift   Flexible Hours   The Night Shift

Working Around the Clock

It used to be that the traditional office workday started at nine in the morning and ended at five in the afternoon. Flash forward to today. Because business can be conducted at any time thanks to the Internet and other electronic devices, the traditional workday is expanding through the evening and even into the night. Your next job could start while most people are going to sleep for the night!

_____

Lasting from four in the afternoon to midnight, this shift is worked by approximately 4 million people in the United States. There are many reasons why people choose to work this nontraditional shift. Parents can set up their work schedule to avoid the high costs of day care – while one parent works, the other parent can care for the children at home. Additionally, jobs with nontraditional hours generally pay better wages. However, the most common reason workers give for working nontraditional hours is that the job demands it. For example, doctors and police officers have to be available around the clock.

_____

Sometimes referred to as the graveyard shift, this shift begins at eleven at night and ends at seven in the morning. Although most of the people working this shift are blue-collar workers such as factory workers or security guards, white-collar workers such as computer programmers and financial analysts can be found at their desks at this time, too. Over a six-year period in the 1990s, the number of white-collar workers working this shift increased by over 11 percent. Because business is being conducted globally across many time zones, it's necessary for workers to be available around the clock.

_____

For those who want to work more traditional hours, but who would like some flexibility in their schedules, working for a company that offers the opportunity to choose when to start the workday is a great option. As long as workers put in the amount of time their employers ask of them, the workers can choose what time to begin their workdays. Some workers prefer to begin their days early, while others prefer to start later. For example, a parent might choose to begin his or her day at ten o'clock instead of nine in order to get children ready for school.

B Read the article again. Then correct the false sentences.

1. Jobs with ~~traditional~~ *nontraditional* hours usually pay better salaries.

2. Working nontraditional hours is always inconvenient for families.

3. In the 1990s, fewer white-collar workers started working the night shift.

4. Today, business is conducted globally between set hours.

5. With flexible hours, employees choose the amount of time they work.

2 *Please consider me.*

Writing

A Read the application letter. Then complete it with the expressions in the box.

Dear	in the *Oakland Journal News*	Sincerely,
Enclosure	Night-Shift Baker	Thank you for your time and consideration.

(1) _____ Mr. Chen,

(2) Re: _____

I am applying for the Night-Shift Baker position you advertised on October 28
(3) _____ . I am currently a third-year student at the Oakland
School of Culinary Arts, and baking is my passion.

While I don't have a lot of experience in commercial baking, I had a part-time job baking in my
school's cafeteria. I was responsible for baking bread and rolls for over 200 students and faculty
members every weekend. I am a diligent worker, and I think I would be an asset to your
company. I have included my résumé for your review.

I would welcome the chance to speak with you at your convenience. I can be reached at
888-555-2387 from 8 a.m. to 1 p.m. every day. (4) _____

(5) _____

Glenn Cross

(6) _____

B Write an application letter for a job you'd really like to have. Include a subject
line, opening paragraph, middle paragraph, closing paragraph, and ending.

Unit 12 Progress chart

Mark the boxes below to rate your progress. ☑ = I know how to . . . ? = I need to review how to . . .	To review, go back to these pages in the Student's Book.
Grammar ☐ use *What* clauses and long noun phrases as subjects	118 and 119
☐ talk about the future with the future continuous and future perfect	120 and 121
Vocabulary ☐ use at least 20 new words to talk about careers	120 and 121
Conversation strategies ☐ introduce what I say with expressions like *The best part is* . . .	122
☐ introduce ideas with *I don't know if* . . .	123
Writing ☐ write an application letter	125

Illustration credits

Chuck Gonzales: 54, 55, 94
Frank Montagna: 52, 67, 76, 78, 79
Marilena Perilli: 58, 59, 70, 71, 93

Greg White: 61, 69
Terry Wong: 50, 62, 63, 90

Photography credits

60 (*clockwise from top left*) ©Punchstock; ©Punchstock; ©Corbis; ©Getty Images
66 ©Peter Menzel
67 ©Punchstock
74 (*top to bottom*) ©ABC/Everett Collection; ©Jose Luis Pelaez Inc./Corbis; ©Zac Macaulay/Getty Images
75 (*clockwise from top right*) ©Punchstock; ©Punchstock; ©Wayne Eardley/Masterfile; ©Punchstock; ©Paul Thomas/Getty Images

77 (*clockwise from top right*) ©Luca Bruno/AP Wide World Photos; ©Steve Azzara/Corbis; ©INFGoff/Newscom; ©20th Century Fox Film Corp./Everett Collection; ©Keline Howard/Corbis Sygma; ©The Kobal Collection
80 (*left to right*) ©Nancy Kaszerman/Newscom; ©Peter Kramer/Getty Images
85 ©Sue Wilson/Alamy
86 ©Randy Faris/Corbis

Text credits

Notes

Notes

Notes